My Life in the Wild
PenGuin

writer **Meredith Costain**

illustrator **Gary Hanna**

KINGFISHER
NEW YORK

I am an emperor penguin.

I am chubby and tall, with short, stubby wings.
My home is Antarctica, a land of ice and snow.
I cannot fly, but I can dive and swim.
Let me tell you my story.

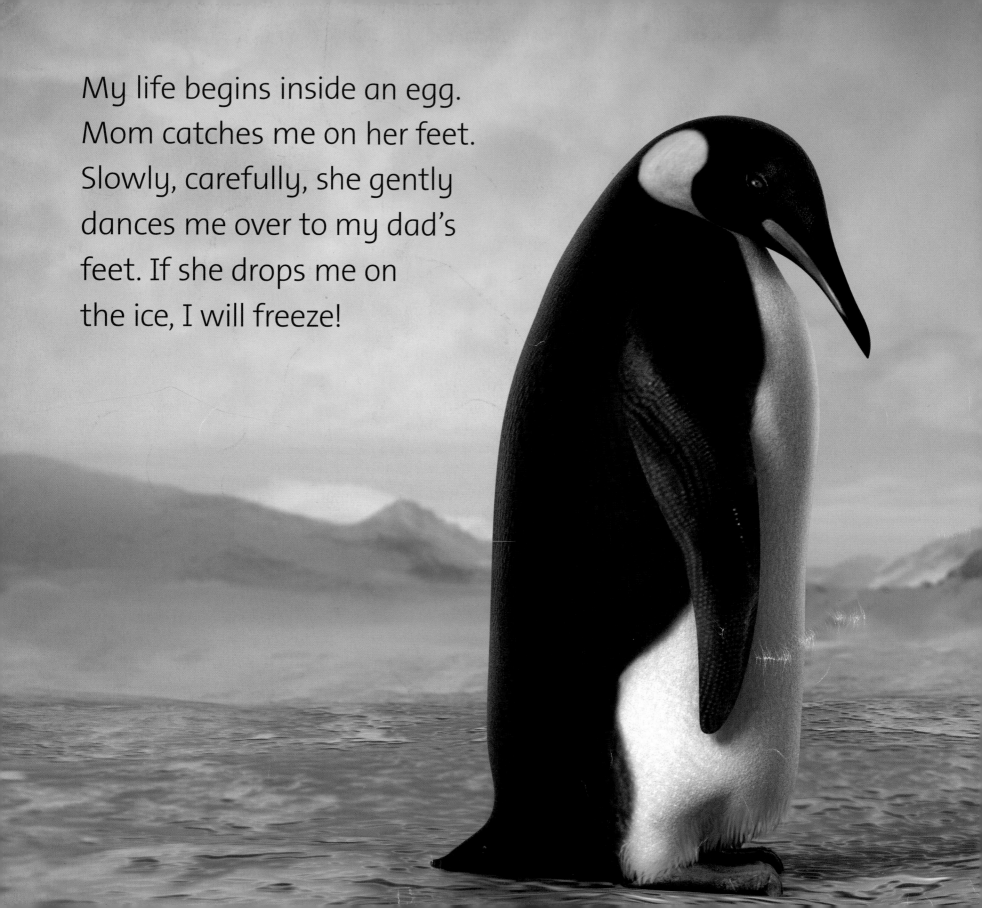

My life begins inside an egg.
Mom catches me on her feet.
Slowly, carefully, she gently
dances me over to my dad's
feet. If she drops me on
the ice, I will freeze!

Mom has left on the long trek to her
favorite feeding ground in the sea.
Dad looks after me while she's away.

I perch in my egg on top of his feet,
protected by his warm body.

The days are growing shorter and colder.
Dad huddles together with a group
of other fathers, turning their backs
to the icy wind.

They take turns standing in the middle.
It's much, much warmer in there!

It's time to leave my egg.
I poke a small hole in the
top with my sharp beak.
Then I chip, chip, chip
away until the top
comes off.

Mom is here, back from the ocean, waiting to greet me. Now it is Dad's turn to feed.

I'm finally big enough to leave Mom's feet. I snuggle together with the other chicks, waiting for our parents to bring us our dinner.

Two family members stay close, watching the sky for hungry giant seabirds.

Here come our moms and dads, back from the sea. I call and call for my mother. The other chicks call too.

Finally, Mom finds me.
She spits a mouthful
of mushy fish straight
into my beak.

It's time for my first swim. I line up with my friends. Splash! One by one we dive into the icy water.

My friend screeches a warning. A leopard seal has followed us in. We duck and weave under the water, desperate to escape.

Terrified, we leap out of the water and back onto the ice. We slither and slide, then scramble across humps of snow.

The hungry leopard seal follows us. But out of the water she's slow and clumsy—too slow to catch any of us!

After four long winters and summers,
my friends and I return to the place
where we were hatched.

It's a long, long way to walk.
We glide across the ice on our bellies
when we get tired. It's fun!

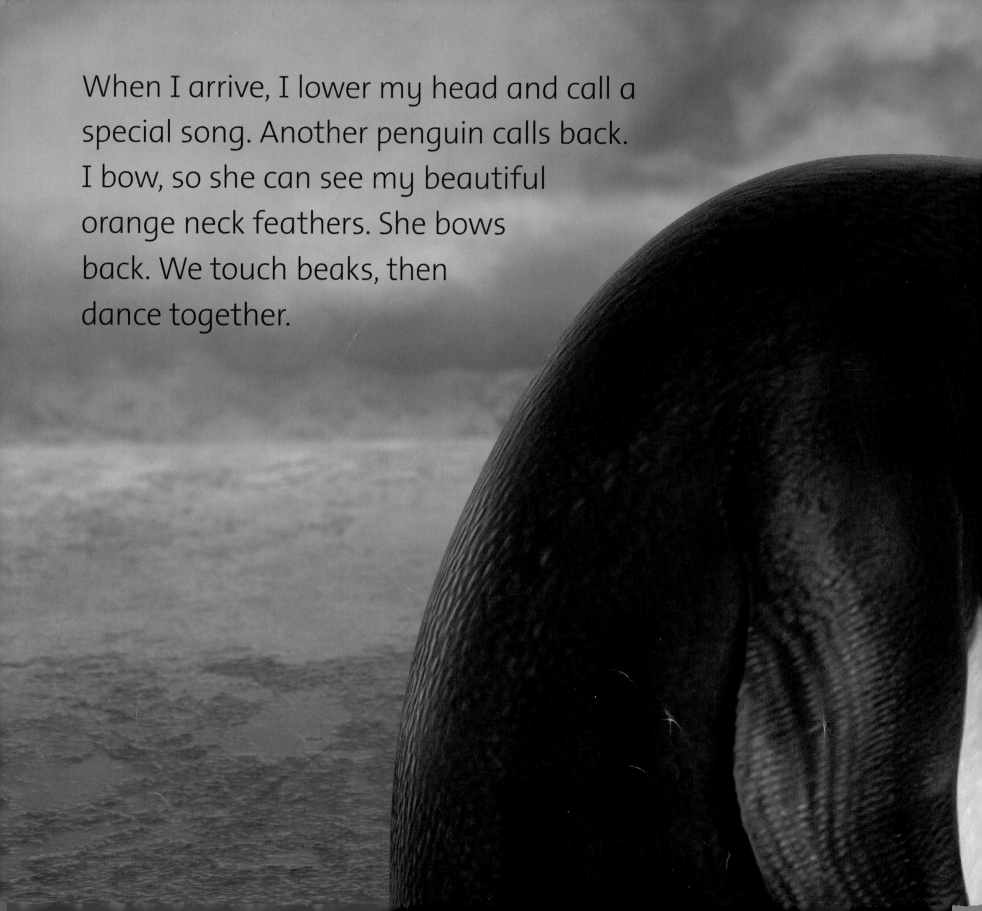

When I arrive, I lower my head and call a special song. Another penguin calls back. I bow, so she can see my beautiful orange neck feathers. She bows back. We touch beaks, then dance together.

After laying our egg, my partner sets off on her long trek back to our feeding ground in the ocean.

I settle down to wait for her return, the egg containing our precious chick safely balanced on my feet.

Did You Know?

The mother lays an egg and passes it to the father.

Emperor penguins live in Antarctica, the coldest place on Earth. Almost all of the continent is covered with ice. When an egg is laid, the mother emperor penguin passes it very carefully to the father's feet. If the egg touches the ice, the chick inside will freeze and die.

The father looks after the egg.

Both the mother and father emperor penguins care for their chick. Once she has laid her egg, the mother returns to the sea to feed, leaving the father behind to look after it. He keeps the egg warm by perching it on his feet and tucking it under a large fold of skin until it is ready to hatch.

Fathers huddle together against the cold.

In winter, temperatures in Antarctica are very low and the winds blow faster than a speeding car. Male penguins huddle together to keep warm. They take turns shuffling from the outside of the huddle into the middle, to save body heat. The penguins in the outside row turn their backs to the cold wind.

The mother returns to feed her newly hatched chick.

It takes two months for the egg to hatch. The chick first makes
a tiny hole in the top of the egg, then pecks away at the
shell until the top comes off. This can take up to three days.
The mother penguin returns from the ocean in time to feed
her chick. The father, who has not eaten for two months,
losing up to half of his body weight, can now go off to feed.

Adult penguins protect the chicks from seabirds.

The chick spends its first three weeks tucked into its mother's brood
pouch, away from the cold ice. When it is old enough to survive on
its own, both parents travel back and forth to the ocean to catch
fish. The fluffy chicks in the nursery huddle together to stay warm.
Two or three adults stay behind to guard them against an attack
by birds such as skuas or giant petrels.

Each penguin makes its own unique sound.

When parents return with food for their chicks, they make their
special call. The chicks answer, guiding their parents through
the thousands of other chicks to find them. Penguin calls can be
heard from 0.6 mile (1 km) away. A penguin feeds its chick by
spitting up the half-digested fish in its stomach into the baby's
mouth. This is called regurgitation.

Did You Know? (continued)

Waterproof feathers allow penguins to swim.

At the end of winter, the ice over the sea begins to melt and break up. The young penguins begin to molt, replacing their fluffy feathers with shiny new waterproof ones. They are now ready for their first swim. They line up and dive off the ice cliffs into the sea near their nursery.

Leopard seals try to catch young penguins.

Leopard seals are fierce hunters and often chase young penguins that are learning to swim. However, they can only catch them in the water—they are much slower and clumsier on land. A penguin's best method of escape is to leap out of the water and back onto the ice shelf.

Penguins move faster in the water than on land.

Penguins are fast and agile swimmers, but they are unable to walk very fast. When they need to cover long distances, they flop down onto their fat tummies and push themselves along with their feet. This is known as tobogganing.

Penguins perform a special dance to find a partner.

At the beginning of winter, adult emperor penguins return to the area where they were hatched. This is called a rookery. Here they choose a mate in a special dance called a mating display. Some emperor penguins keep the same partner for life, while others choose a new mate each season.

The new penguin pair has its first egg.

Three weeks after mating, the female penguin lays a single egg. She then sets off on the long trek back to the ocean to find food, leaving her mate to care for the egg. The cycle of life starts all over again.

Meet the Penguin Family

There are 17 different types, or species, of penguins.
Here are some of the family members.

Emperor penguin

King penguin

Gentoo penguin

Chinstrap penguin

QUIZ

1. Which penguin looks the most like the emperor penguin?

2. Which penguin is the largest?

3. Which penguins have only black and white feathers?

4. Which penguins have black banded markings on their bodies?

Emperor penguin

Scientific name: *Aptenodytes forsteri*

Coat color: black back, white belly, colorful neck feathers

Height: 3.8 feet (1.15 m)

Weight: 66 pounds (30 kg)

Food: fish, krill, and squid

Dive depth: 1,850 feet (565 m)

Breath-holding length: up to 22 minutes

Life span: 20 years

Conservation status: least concern

Habitat: all around the coasts of the Antarctic continent

Where emperor penguins live

South Pole

ANTARCTICA

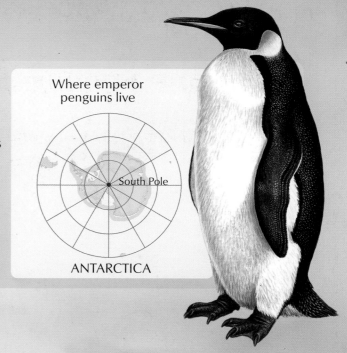

Magellanic penguin

Adélie penguin

Yellow-eyed penguin

Erect-crested penguin

Fiordland penguin

Little penguin

7. Which penguin has colorful eyes?

5. How many different types of penguins can you see here?

9. Which penguin is the smallest?

6. Which penguins have colorful crests?

8. Which penguins have colorful feathers on their necks?

Glossary

brood pouch   a thick flap of tummy skin

continent   a large mass of land

crest   a bunch of feathers on the head

hatch   to break out of the shell

mate   a partner to have a family with

molt   to lose a layer of old feathers or fur

nursery   a place where young are cared for

rookery   a place where birds gather to lay eggs

seabird   a bird that lives near the ocean

unique   the only one of its kind

KINGFISHER
LONDON & NEW YORK

Published in the United States by Kingfisher, 175 Fifth Ave., New York, NY 10010

Kingfisher is an imprint of Macmillan Children's Books, London.
All rights reserved.

Distributed in the U.S. by Macmillan, 175 Fifth Ave., New York, NY 10010

Library of Congress Cataloging-in-Publication data has been applied for.

Kingfisher books are available for special promotions and premiums.

For details contact: Special Markets Department, Macmillan, 175 Fifth Ave., New York, NY 10010.

For more information, please visit www.kingfisherbooks.com

Conceived and produced by
Weldon Owen Pty Ltd
59–61 Victoria Street, McMahons Point
Sydney NSW 2060, Australia
weldonowenpublishing.com

Copyright © 2011 Weldon Owen Pty Ltd

WELDON OWEN PTY LTD

Managing Director Kay Scarlett
Publisher Corinne Roberts
Creative Director Sue Burk
**Senior Vice President,
International Sales** Stuart Laurence
Sales Manager, North America Ellen Towell
**Administration Manager,
International Sales** Kristine Ravn

Editor Shan Wolody
Consultant Professor Phil Whitfield
Design Concept Cooling Brown Ltd
Designers Gabrielle Green, Adam Walker
Design Assistant Emily Spencer
Images Manager Trucie Henderson
Production Director Todd Rechner
Production and Prepress Controller Mike Crowton
Illustrations Gary Hanna/The Art Agency except Meet the Penguin Family pages.

ISBN: 978-0-7534-6724-4

Printed and bound in China by 1010 Printing Int Ltd.

The paper used in the manufacture of this book is sourced from wood grown in sustainable forests. It complies with the Environmental Management System Standard ISO 14001:2004

A WELDON OWEN PRODUCTION